Roy L

FRET
BUSTERS

HARVEST HOUSE PUBLISHERS
EUGENE, OREGON

Cover design by Franke Design and Illustration, Excelsior, Minnesota

Cover illustration © odze / iStock

FRET BUSTERS
Copyright © 2015 Roy Lessin
Published by Harvest House Publishers
Eugene, Oregon 97408
www.harvesthousepublishers.com

ISBN 978-0-7369-5907-0 (pc)
ISBN 978-0-7369-5908-7 (eBook)

Printed in China

18 19 20 21 22 23 / RDS-JH / 10 9 8 7 6 5 4

There are many reasons why we can become worried or anxious as we live in this world. *But there is a greater reason not to!* As you read the following pages, it's my prayer that your faith in God will be strengthened and your love for Him will be deepened.

May His strength be your strength, may His joy be your joy, may His peace be your peace, and may His hope be your hope.

"Love never fails" (1 Corinthians 13:8).

Roy Lessin

Fret Buster 1

"I Am God!"

Lord, You are who You say You are. You do what You say You do. There is no other like You! You are the highest, the greatest, the best. You have no weakness, no lack, and no equal. You are my God. You are my heavenly Father.

I find comfort in Your nearness, security in Your voice, courage in Your strength, hope in Your promises.

You are enough—more than enough! You are with me always. You are my refuge. I am safe in Your care.

Come to Me,
Separate yourself unto Me,
Know Me,
Trust Me…
I am your God.
I dwell with you.
Walk with you.
Welcome you.
You are my child.
I am your Father.

(BASED ON 2 CORINTHIANS 6:16-18)

[The LORD said,]
"I am
Almighty
God."

(Genesis 17:1)

Fret Buster 2

Even Though

Take His hand, even though it means letting go of what you're holding on to.
Please His heart, even though it may not please others.
Wait for His time, even though your desire is to get it done now.
Obey His Word, even though you hear something different that is popular.
Follow His path, even though you see a valley ahead.
Trust His wisdom, even though you want to do it differently.
Give Him praise, even though you're going through something unpleasant.
Be at rest, even though you have every human reason to worry or fear.

Uphold me according to Your word, that I may live; and do not let me be ashamed of my hope. Hold me up, and I shall be safe,

and I shall observe Your statutes continually
(Psalm 119:116-117).

Throughout the Scriptures God proclaims and demonstrates who He is and what He can do. God is all in all! He has no lack, no faults, no weaknesses, no limitations, and no failures. The plan of our salvation is His plan. The work of our salvation is His work. The gift of our salvation is His gift. Every grace comes from Him. All that we have we have freely received from His generous hand.

How should we respond to His greatness and abounding generosity? Our responses are to be with Him, learn about Him, love Him, and *trust Him with all our hearts.*

If we obey God without fully trusting Him and knowing His heart, we will struggle in our obedience. A nineteenth-century writer got it right when she wrote, "Perfect obedience would be perfect happiness, if only we had full confidence in the authority we were obeying." We can *fully* put our trust in what God has said and promised, who He is, what He has done, what He is doing, and what He will do. He will not fail us because there is no failure in Him.

Fret Buster 3

There will never be a time when you will find God's power inadequate, His love indifferent, or His grace insufficient.

> The Spirit and the bride say, "Come!" Let those who hear this say, "Come!" Let those who are thirsty come! Let those who want the water of life take it as a gift (Revelation 22:17 GW).

God gives to you freely out of the riches of His grace, the bounty of His goodness, the kindness of His favor, the depths of His love, the tender ministry of His Spirit, and the blessings that abound to you in His Son, Jesus Christ—all of which have no limitations and can never be depleted. By faith receive from Him today for He is the endless supply!

Needy?

Come and ask.

Seeking?

Come and find.

Thirsty?

Come and drink.

Hungry?

Come and dine.

Hurt?

Come and heal.

Weary?

Come and rest.

Fret Buster 4

Stop worrying about what you will eat, drink, or wear. Isn't life more than food and the body more than clothes? Look at the birds. They don't plant, harvest, or gather the harvest into barns. Yet, your heavenly Father feeds them. Aren't you worth more than they?

Can any of you add a single hour to your life by worrying? And why worry about clothes? Notice how the flowers grow in the field. They never work or spin yarn for clothes. But I say that not even Solomon in all his majesty was dressed like one of these flowers…So how much more will he clothe you people who have so little faith? *Don't ever worry* and say, "What are we going to eat?" or "What are we going to drink?" or "What are we going to wear?" Everyone is concerned about these things, and your heavenly Father certainly knows you need all of them. But first, be concerned about his kingdom and what has his approval.

Then all these things will be provided for you (Matthew 6:25-33 GW).

Needy

Jesus, You spoke the word and the storm became still (Mark 4:39). *Lord, I need a word like that.*

Jesus, You healed—those who touched the hem of Your garment were made whole (Mark 6:56). *Lord, I need a healing like that.*

Jesus, You gave the spiritually hungry the bread of life (John 6:48-51). *Lord, I need to be fed like that.*

Jesus, You placed Your hands upon the children and blessed them (Mark 10:16). *Lord, I need to be touched like that.*

Jesus, You blessed the bread and the wine as You communed with Your disciples (Mark 14:22-24). *Lord, I need fellowship like that.*

Jesus, You go before Your sheep, and they follow You (John 10:2-4). *Lord, I need guidance like that.*

Jesus, You promised Your peace and said don't be troubled or afraid (John 14:27). *Lord, I need assurance like that.*

Jesus, You lived to please Your Father (John 8:29). *Lord, I need a relationship like that.*

Fret Buster 5

Confidence is not based on you having all the resources needed to take care of yourself. True confidence is based on the truth that *God is faithful*.

A Benediction

> I pray that you may prosper in every way and [that your body] may keep well, even as [I know] your soul keeps well and prospers (3 John 1:2 AMP, brackets in original).

May all things be well with you.

May you do well,

choose well,

think well,

love well,

serve well,

feel well,

and stay well

as you continue to trust
in the only One
who does all things well.

Fret Buster 6

How is it possible to live free from worry? Living free from worry doesn't mean that our needs will disappear. It means our needs will be met by God, who is our Provider. When we stay focused on what our needs are, we open our hearts to worry; when we stay focused on who God is, we open our hearts to peace.

Thankfully, we have a Master who not only gives us rest *from* our labor, but He also gives us rest *in* our labor. We have a Master who *is* our rest.

> Jesus said, "Let's go off by ourselves to a quiet place and *rest awhile*" (Mark 6:31 NLT).

> Come to me, all of you who are weary and carry heavy burdens, and *I will give you rest* (Matthew 11:28 NLT).

> Rest *in the* LORD (Psalm 37:7).

God said,
I am here with you.
All that I am is here…
All My love is here.
All My goodness is here.
All My righteousness is here.
All My grace is here.
All My strength is here.
All My ways, My works, My wisdom,
My wonders are here!
Is there anything too hard for Me?

Fret Buster 7

"Will Be"

> "Will be!"
> Not "might be."
> Not "could be."

What a blessed reality; what a magnificent truth; what a hope-filled promise from the God of all hope. His "will be" is our hope in dark times, troubled times, uncertain times, changing times. So what "will be"?

> He will be!
> His return will be!
> His reign will be!
> His righteousness will be.
> Your place with Him will be.
> Your inheritance in Him will be.

> The night is almost gone;
> the *day of salvation* will soon be here.
> Romans 13:12 NLT

Keep this

HOPE

in your heart.

Keep the

DAY

of

SALVATION

in your planner.

Keep this

LIGHT

in your eye.

Fret Buster 8

I know the one in whom I trust, and I am sure that he is able to guard what I have entrusted to him until the day of his return (2 Timothy 1:12 NLT).

Prayer of Release

Heavenly Father, I release to You the burdens that I've been carrying—burdens that You never intended for me to carry. I cast my cares on You—all my worries and all my fears. You've told me to not be anxious about anything, but, instead, to bring everything to You in prayer with thankfulness.

Father, calm my restless spirit, quiet my anxious heart, and still my troubling thoughts with the assurance that You are in control. I choose to let go of my grip on the things I've been hanging on to. With open hands I come to You. I release to Your will all that I am trying to manipulate. I release to Your authority all that I am trying to control. I release to Your timing all that I have been striving to make happen.

I thank You for Your promise to sustain me, preserve

me, and guard all that I entrust to Your keeping. Protect my heart and mind with Your peace—the peace that passes all understanding.

Father, may Your will be done in my life in Your time and in Your way. Amen.

(Psalm 55:22; 1 Peter 5:7; Philippians 4:6; Matthew 6:25-34; Isaiah 26:3; Philippians 4:7; Luke 11:2)

When we are careful to instantly let go of all needless worries and restless thoughts, then we shall find ourselves on plateaus of peace.

FÉNELON

Fret Buster 9

The likeness of the firmament above the heads of the living creatures was like the color of an awesome crystal, stretched out over their heads...And *when they stood still, they let down their wings.* A voice came from above the firmament that was over their heads; whenever they stood, they let down their wings (Ezekiel 1:22-25).

"Flapping wings" is a good picture of activity. It can be good activity—even activity in doing the Lord's work. However, we all need times when we quiet ourselves before the Lord. "Letting down our wings" means quieting ourselves and being still before the Lord so we can hear His voice. It's a very good thing to be still and know that He is God. We need to become good listeners.

Behold, God is my salvation, I will trust and not be afraid (Isaiah 12:2).

HAVE FAITH

in His wisdom to
guide,

in His love to
direct,

in His power to
sustain,

in His faithfulness to
fulfill.

Fret Buster 10

Letting Go

What do we do with the things we can't fix, the decisions we can't control, the events we can't attend, the opportunities we can't respond to, and the circumstances we can't change? Should we get angry, frustrated, anxious, disappointed, grumbly, or discouraged? Thankfully, there is a better response! The response is like a two-sided coin. On one side the coin says "Let Go" on the other side it says "Let God."

"Letting go" is when you find release;
"Letting God" is when your heart finds peace.

"Letting go" is when you seek His best;
"Letting God" is when your heart finds rest.

"Letting Go" is when you choose His will;
"Letting God" is when your heart is still.

"God, I have let go, but I'm falling!" I cried out in fear. *"Do not be troubled,"* He lovingly replied. *"I am underneath you, and you are falling into My everlasting arms!"*

God is too *powerful* to lead you to a place of defeat;
Too *wise* to bring wrong things into your life;
Too *caring* to leave you without comfort;
Too *observant* to miss a detail;
Too *loving* to withhold anything that is good.

> Casting the whole of your care [all your anxieties, all your worries, all your concerns, once and for all] on Him, for He cares for you affectionately and cares about you watchfully (1 Peter 5:7 AMP, brackets in original).

Once we give our worries to God, He doesn't want us to worry about how He is going to take care of them. He is God almighty. He knows how to take care of us. We can leave the details to Him.

Fret Buster 11

A Quiet Heart

We can learn something important from the way of a mother with a frightened child. A child's response to fear is not a whimper. It's a wail. The mother's response is not casual or indifferent. No, it is instant and intense. Love moves into action, and not with just explanations or reasoning, but with everything within its power to quiet, to comfort, and to reassure. The arms of a mother's embrace speak louder than any words the child can hear in that moment of fear.

The mother's voice is also soothing. "Shhh, it's okay now. Mommy's here. It's okay." These words are all the child needs to know. Her gentle words and loving arms bring the reassurance that helps the child become calm.

God's words can be likened to the words of a caring mother to her fearful child. The language in Psalm 46:10-11 is simple, the words are few, the impact is instant, the result is profound. His words tell us all we need to know to settle down, still our fears, quiet our hearts, and reassure us. Hear His encouraging voice: "Be still. Release all your concerns and quiet your heart. *You are okay. I am here. You are safe in the shelter of My arms.*"

BE STILL,

— and know that —

I AM GOD...

The LORD
of hosts
is with us;
the God of Jacob is

our refuge.

(Psalm 46:10-11)

Fret Buster 12

> An aged, weary woman, carrying a heavy basket, got aboard a train, and when seated she did not let go of her heavy basket. The kind voice of a man sitting next to her spoke these words, "Lay down your burden, madam, the train will carry both it and you."

> J.H. JOWETT, *THE SILVER LINING*

In this illustration, the aged woman's basket and its contents were not bad things. The basket may have contained the food items needed to feed her family that day. It was the *weight* of the basket that made the woman weary.

Is there something in your life that has become a burden? It may be a good thing, and the right thing for you to do, but there may be a weight associated with it that is making you weary. The Lord may not want you to cast away the good thing, but He does want you to cast the care of it on Him. He wants you to let Him carry it.

Perhaps the weight is associated with your job. The Lord may want you to keep the job but not carry the weight of "striving in your work to get ahead."

Perhaps the weight is associated with a ministry. The Lord may want you to continue in that ministry but not carry the weight of "trying to please people."

Perhaps the weight is associated with a difficult situation. The Lord may want you to press through the difficulty but not carry the weight of "doing it in your own strength."

The Lord desires to release you from every burden that would weigh you down, make your heart heavy, or rob you of the strength you need to do His will. He will sustain you. He is able to carry both you and the weight of your burden!

> Cast your burden on the LORD, and He shall sustain you; He shall never permit the righteous to be moved (Psalm 55:22).

Fret Buster 13

We have *peace* with God through our Lord
Jesus Christ (Romans 5:1).

Father, I have received peace *from* You and peace
with You because of Your Son's sacrifice for me. It's
amazing to know that all is well with my soul, that all
has been made right in my relationship with You, that
I have been accepted in the beloved and adopted into
Your family.

You are the God of peace, the provider of peace, and
the One who maintains my peace. Your peace is my
safe place, my sheltered place, my abiding place.

Your peace is my pathway. May every step I take be
guided by Your peace; may every decision I make be
governed by Your peace; may every act of service I do
be guarded by Your peace. Lord, let Your peace mark
my footsteps, empower my words, and shield my heart.

Peace is in Your voice, peace is in Your heart, peace
is in Your kingdom, peace is in Your truth, peace is in
Your purposes. Thank You for keeping me in Your perfect peace.

I can

GO

when God sends me,

I can

REJOICE

when standing still.

I am

PATIENT &
CONTENTED,

when I'm resting in His will.

Fret Buster 14

There is a grace God gives when it's His time for us to do His will. There is a grace that He gives us when we are waiting on His will to be done. His grace includes the fruit of patience and the peace of contentment. Patience says, "I can wait for His timing." Contentment says, "I am at peace with the way things are at the moment." Patience allows us to wait without striving; contentment allows us to wait without complaint.

> Ask, and you will receive. Search, and you will find. Knock, and the door will be opened for you. Everyone who asks will receive. The one who searches will find, and for the one who knocks, the door will be opened. If your child asks you for bread, would any of you give him a stone? Or if your child asks for a fish, would you give him a snake? Even though you're evil, you know how to give good gifts to your children. So how much more will your Father in heaven give good things to those who ask Him? (Matthew 7:7-11 GW).

Though everyone fails you, *God remains faithful* (2 Timothy 2:13).

Though everyone speaks lies, *God remains true* (Romans 3:3-4 GW).

Though all things lose their luster, *God remains glorious* (2 Corinthians 3:8-11).

Though all would forsake you, *God remains with you* (Haggai 2:4-5).

Though the world grows exceedingly troubled, *God remains in control* (John 16:33).

Fret Buster 15

For we know in part and we prophesy in part…For now we see in a mirror, dimly, but then face to face. Now I know in part, but then I shall know just as I also am known (1 Corinthians 13:9,12).

Be patient. We don't need to know everything right now. In this life we won't be able to resolve every question, solve every problem, or understand every situation. In time, everything will be made clear. Things won't always be the way they are right now. We don't need to fret over God's timetable. We will inherit all the promises of God through faith and patience. God knows how and when to bring about change. Trust His timing.

Are not two sparrows sold for a copper coin? And not one of them falls to the ground apart from your Father's will. But the very hairs of your head are all numbered. Do not fear therefore; you are of more value than many sparrows (Matthew 10:29-31).

If you ever see

a lily toiling

—— or ——

a bird storing up food in a barn,

you will know the time to

worry

has arrived.

(Based on Matthew 6:26-28)

Fret Buster 16

The only reason to fear or worry is *if* the Lord had said…

1. Lay up treasures on earth, for there are no treasures in heaven.

2. Be anxious about life, for God doesn't know anything about you.

3. The most important thing in life is what you possess, so get more.

4. Your Father in heaven doesn't care for you; you are on your own.

5. Seek what the world seeks; that is where true values are.

6. Be anxious about tomorrow; it's good to have things pile up.

7. God doesn't look after the practical details of life; save yourself.

Since He didn't say these things, continue to walk in peace.

> Let your character or moral disposition be free from love of money [including greed, avarice, lust, and craving for earthly possessions] and be satisfied with your present [circumstances and with what you have]; for He [God] Himself has said, I will not in any way fail you nor give you up nor leave you without support. [I will] not, [I will] not, [I will] not in any degree leave you helpless nor forsake nor let [you] down (relax My hold on you)! [Assuredly not!] So we take comfort and are encouraged and confidently and boldly say, The Lord is my Helper; I will not be seized with alarm [I will not fear or dread or be terrified]. What can man do to me? (Hebrews 13:5-6 AMP, brackets in original).

Fret Buster 17

Uphold me according to Your word, that I may live; and do not let me be ashamed of my hope. Hold me up, and I shall be safe, and I shall observe Your statutes continually (Psalm 119:116-17).

You can count on God.

His words are truth; He cannot lie.

His character is flawless;

He does what He says He will do.

He never fails. He never errs.

The

LORD
Himself
will fight
FOR YOU.

Just stay calm.

(Exodus 14:14 NLT)

Fret Buster 18

What has the Lord asked of you? Is it time for you to step out? To be still? To let go? When you know the next step God wants you to take, you must take it in the full confidence of faith. Never put limits on yourself as to how much you will obey. Never put limits on God regarding how much He can do.

Anna J. Lindgren said, "He who depends *wholly* and *unconditionally* on God becomes an agent for unlimited possibilities." What is possible for you today as one who believes in the Lord? Jesus said, "All things are possible to him who believes" (Mark 9:23). Place and keep your complete and unconditional trust in the Lord, so you can joyfully walk with Him along the path of unlimited possibilities.

Safe Pastures

We all need *sanctified* imaginations. It's easy for us to fret and let our imaginations run wild. In reality, most things don't happen the way we imagined them. The Bible doesn't tell us to live by our imaginations. Our imaginations can be a fast track to worry. Worry says, "What happens to me seems out of my control." Faith says, "My life is in God's hands, and He is in control."

If our imagination runs free, it will soon run wild. Without being under the control of the Holy Spirit, our imagination can easily mislead us. Unchecked imagination can quickly take us down the road of anxiety and expose us to a wide variety of fears. We need to yield control of our imagination to the Holy Spirit. He will keep our imagination feeding in the safe pastures depicted in Psalm 23. Jesus, our Good Shepherd, will lead our minds to still waters and quiet resting places.

> The LORD is my shepherd; I shall not want (Psalm 23:1).

Fret Buster 19

He who did not spare His own Son, but delivered Him up for us all, how shall He not with Him also freely give us all things? (Romans 8:32).

God did not give up on us when we didn't know Him, and He will certainly not give up on us now that we are His.

Listen to Me [says the Lord], O house of Jacob, and all the remnant of the house of Israel, you who have been borne by Me from your birth, carried from the womb: Even to your old age I am He, and even to hair white with age will I carry you. I have made, and I will bear; yes, I will carry and will save you (Isaiah 46:3-4 AMP, brackets in original).

There's no need
to try and figure everything out.
God is omniscient.

There's no need
to worry about where you are
or where you are going.
God is omnipresent.

There's no need
to do things in your own strength.
God is omnipotent.

Fret Buster 20

Take my yoke upon you. Let me teach you, because I am humble and gentle at heart, and you will find rest for your souls. For my yoke is easy to bear, and the burden I give you is light (Matthew 11:29-30 NLT).

When you are yoked to Jesus, you *are not* yoked to restlessness, strife, or worry.

Anxiety in the heart of man causes depression (Proverbs 12:25).

Anxiety is contrary to the very character and name of God, especially when we call Him "heavenly Father." If you find that you're anxious about something, ask yourself if you've prayed about it and fully committed it to the Lord. If you have and are still anxious, thank God in your heart and in your prayers for being in control of the situation. Prayer, commitment, and thanksgiving open the door to God's peace. *And His peace often arrives* before *the answer comes.*

When you are weary, come to Me.
I will refresh you.
When you are troubled, come to Me.
I will quiet you.
When you are anxious, come to Me.
I will reassure you.
When you are restless, come to Me.
I will speak peace to you.
When you are uncertain of My love,
come to Me.
I will share My heart with you.

Fret Buster 21

The great evangelical preacher Octavius Winslow (1808–1878) shared this insightful wisdom:

> Let the precious truth divest your mind of all needless, anxious care for the present or the future. Exercising simple faith in God, "do not be anxious about anything" [Philippians 4:6]. Learn to be content with your present lot, with God's dealings with, and His disposal of, you. You are just where His providence has, in its inscrutable but all-wise and righteous decision, placed you. It may be a position painful, irksome, trying, but it is right...Only aim to glorify Him in it.

> Wherever you are placed, God has a work for you to do, a purpose through you to be accomplished, in which He blends your happiness with His glory...

> Live a life of daily dependence upon God. It saves from many a desponding feeling, from many a corroding care, from many an anxious thought, from many a sleepless night.

Father,

you are the God of peace—

peace transcending,

peace defending,

peace befriending,

peace descending,

peace unending.

Fret Buster 22

Be anxious for nothing, but in everything by prayer and supplication, with thanksgiving, let your requests be made known to God (Philippians 4:6).

How much peace does it take to balance out the anxiety in our lives? No amount of peace can balance anxiety! There is no balancing point. God wants the peace-to-anxiety ratio in our lives to be 100 percent peace and 0 percent anxiety.

A Prayer of Peace

Lord Jesus, I thank You that You are the Prince of peace, and that You've promised to give me Your peace. I receive Your peace—the peace that passes all understanding, the peace that assures me of Your presence, the peace that confirms Your love, the peace that guards my every thought and every emotion.

Thank You that You came not to trouble me, but to give me rest; not to confuse me, but to give me clarity; not to bind me, but to free me; not to stress me, but to quiet me. Thank You for Your peace that endures the trials, overcomes in battles, conquers foes, and keeps me steady through storms.

Thank You, Lord, for Your complete peace, for Your perfect peace, for Your peace that keeps my heart from being troubled. Come now and fill me with Your presence. Thank You for the perfect peace that flows when I put my trust in You. Let it wash over me and flood my innermost being. Show me the ways of peace, keep me on the paths of peace, guide me in the decisions that lead to peace. Jesus, be my peace today.

(Isaiah 9:6; John 14:27; Luke 1:79; Philippians 4:6-7; Psalm 29:11; 55:18; 85:8; Isaiah 26:3; 32:17; 54:10; 57:19; Romans 14:17; 15:33; Colossians 3:15)

Fret Buster 23

How much of your cares and concerns can you cast on the Lord? All of it! All worry, all anxiety, all concerns, all burdens. Do it once and for all, and then get out of the worrying business. Envision hanging a banner over your heart that reads, "Under the Management of the Prince of Peace!"

Be at peace. God has not forgotten you!

Sing, O heavens!
Be joyful, O earth!
And break out in singing, O mountains!
For the LORD has comforted His people,
and will have mercy on His afflicted.
But Zion said, "The LORD has forsaken me,
and my Lord has forgotten me."
Can a woman forget her nursing child,
And not have compassion on the son of her womb?
Surely they may forget,
Yet I will not forget you.
See, I have inscribed you on the palms of My hands;
Your walls are continually before Me.

ISAIAH 49:13-16

His name will be called...

PRINCE

—— of ——

PEACE.

(Isaiah 9:6)

Fret Buster 24

The Enemy of Peace Has Been Defeated

Your biggest enemy against peace isn't finances, pressures of life, difficulties, or circumstances of any sort. Your biggest enemy of peace is the devil. He wants to keep you off balance, uncertain, insecure, and troubled about anything and everything that is happening to you or going on around you.

Before you knew Christ, the devil told you there was no hope for you. When you heard the gospel, the devil told you that God couldn't be trusted. When you put your trust in the Lord, the devil told you that you didn't trust God enough. The devil's plan is simple: He wants to keep you from the truth by tempting you to believe a lie. Lies are thieves that come to steal away the peace of God.

God's will is to keep you in perfect peace. Always stay on God's side, and always stay in God's truth. Knowing and believing God's truth empowers you to resist, reject, and refuse to listen to your biggest enemy of peace—the devil.

Keep your mind clear, and be alert. Your

opponent the devil is prowling around like a roaring lion as he looks for someone to devour. Be firm in the faith and resist him (1 Peter 5:8-9 GW).

Hear His Voice

Jesus said that He is the good shepherd, and His sheep hear His voice (John 10:11,14,16). Here are two ways to tell His voice from the voice of the enemy:

- Jesus doesn't nag, confuse, tease, mock, bully, torment, belittle, degrade, discourage, destroy, harass, or falsify.

- Jesus frees, heals, releases, renews, restores, reassures, encourages, comforts, upholds, assures, affirms, edifies, and gives life.

The sheep follow [the Shepherd] because they recognize his voice. They won't follow a stranger. Instead, they will run away from a stranger because they don't recognize his voice (John 10:4-5 GW).

Fret Buster 25

The peace the world gives comes from the things the world has to offer. Since everything the world has to offer is temporary, the peace the world gives quickly passes away. The peace that Jesus gives comes from who He is. And everything Jesus is lasts forever!

> The helper, the Holy Spirit, whom the Father will send in my name, will teach you everything. He will remind you of everything that I have ever told you. I'm leaving you peace. I'm giving you my peace. I don't give you the kind of peace that the world gives. So don't be troubled or cowardly (John 14:26-27 GW).

Peace
is not the
absence
of
conflict,
but the
presence
of
JESUS.

Fret Buster 26

Has God ever forgotten you? Will He forget you now? Never!

> Can a mother forget her nursing child? Can she feel no love for the child she has borne? But even if that were possible, I [the LORD] would not forget you! (Isaiah 49:15 NLT).

> You have searched me, LORD, and you know me. You know when I sit and when I rise; you perceive my thoughts from afar. You discern my going out and my lying down; you are familiar with all my ways (Psalm 139:1-3).

May You Receive from the Lord...

If you're *worried*, may you receive the Lord's *peace*:

> Peace I leave with you; My [own] peace I now give and bequeath to you. Not as the world gives do I give to you. Do not let your hearts be troubled, neither let them

be afraid. [Stop allowing yourselves to be agitated and disturbed; and do not permit yourselves to be fearful and intimidated and cowardly and unsettled] (John 14:27 AMP, brackets in original).

If you're *wondering*, may you receive the Lord's *clarity*:

Let my cry come before You, O LORD; give me understanding according to Your word (Psalm 119:169).

If you're *wandering*, may you receive the Lord's *direction*:

[The LORD says,] "I will bring the blind by a way that they know not; I will lead them in paths that they have not known. I will make darkness into light before them and make uneven places into a plain. These things I have determined to do [for them]; and I will not leave them forsaken" (Isaiah 42:16 AMP, brackets in original).

Fret Buster 27

> I am the Lord, the God of all flesh; is there
> anything too hard for Me? (Jeremiah 32:27
> AMP).

Surrender to God's will today to take the dread out of tomorrow. The psalmist wrote, "I have not seen the righteous forsaken" (Psalm 37:25). Find your rest in God today, and let Him assume the responsibility for all your tomorrows.

> It is the Lord Who goes before you; He will
> [march] with you; He will not fail you or let
> you go or forsake you; [let there be no cow-
> ardice or flinching, but] fear not, neither
> become broken [in spirit—depressed, dis-
> mayed, and unnerved with alarm] (Deuter-
> onomy 31:8 AMP, brackets in original).

It is
true!

The One who is *before* you
and with you will not fail you.

The One who is before you
and *with* you will not fail you.

The One who is before you
and with you *will not fail* you.

The One who is before you
and with you will not fail *you*.

Fret Buster 28

> Gideon built an altar there unto the LORD,
> and called it Jehovah-shalom (Judges 6:24).

The Jewish word "shalom" is much more than a casual social greeting. It is also a prayer, a blessing, a deep desire, and a benediction. Shalom is packed with the full blessing of God. In Hebrew, the word has many significant meanings that are used throughout the Scriptures. The following blessing is a compilation of those meanings.

> May you be whole in body, soul, and spirit as a result of being in harmony with God's will and purpose for your life. May His peace be your covering, may your heart know His fullness, and by His mighty power may you know victory over every enemy.

> May God bring to pass the deepest desires of your heart.
> May you know the healing power of His presence

and the restoration of every broken
relationship.
Through His sufficiency,
may every need that you face
be met by His limitless resources.
May His covenant promises be fulfilled in your
life and in your family.
May He bring you the greatest measure of contentment and the deepest satisfaction that
your heart can possibly know.

The LORD bless you and keep you;
the LORD make His face shine upon you,
and be gracious to you;
the LORD lift up His countenance upon
you and give you peace
(Numbers 6:24-26).

Fret Buster 29

A Prayer of Trust

Lord, I trust in You. I believe in You. I hope in You. You are my confidence and my assurance. I lean on You because You are my Rock. I depend on You because You are my Provider. I delight in You because You are the joy of my life. My heart rests in You. My faith responds to You. My soul rejoices in You.

You are the true God who cannot lie and will never fail. You are the Lord, the almighty God, the Creator of all things. You are my Lord, my God, and my Maker.

You are my Keeper, and I am secure in You. You are my heavenly Father, and I am cared for by You. You are my Counselor, and I am guided by You. You are my shelter, and I am safe.

I trust You in my life—the wisdom of Your ways, the blessings of Your favor, the sufficiency of Your grace, the power of Your Spirit, and the endurance that comes from Your strength. I trust You. My mind trusts in You. My will trusts in You. My soul trusts in You. From the depths of my being, I trust You. Amen.

LORD,

I trust You *for* all things.
I trust You *with* all things.
I trust You *in* all things.
I trust You *through* all things.
I trust You *above* all things.

Fret Buster 30

You had faith in the creature, and it disappointed you; in earthly good, and it faded away; in your own heart, and it deceived you. Now, have faith in God! Call upon him in your trouble, try Him in your trial, trust Him in your need, and see if He will not honor the faith that honors Him. "Have faith in God"—oh, what sweet words of Jesus, spoken to allure your weary spirit to its divine and blessed rest.

OCTAVIUS WINSLOW

The praying spirit breathe,
The watching power impart,
From all entanglements beneath
Call off my anxious heart.
My feeble mind sustain,
By worldly thoughts oppressed;
Appear, and bid me turn again
To my eternal rest.

CHARLES WESLEY

God's voice is the best voice to hear, the most assuring voice to trust, the clearest voice to follow, the wisest voice to obey, the most recognizable voice to run to. Let the voice of God quiet your heart.

> I will hear what God the LORD will speak,
> for He will speak peace to His people (Psalm 85:8).

Father in heaven, I entrust my future into Your hands because You are the beginning and the end. You know the end from the beginning so I entrust my hopes into Your hands. You never lie so I entrust my labors into Your hands. You are my exceedingly great reward so I entrust my life into Your hands. You are the One who does all things well.

Fret Buster 31

Who am I? I am God's child! I am a child of grace and mercy. Jesus looked upon me and came to me with healing in His wings—He saw an empty cup and filled it; He saw an unclean vessel and cleansed it; He saw a restless soul and brought it peace; He saw a lost sheep and brought it home; He saw a vain life and gave it meaning; He saw a selfish heart and baptized it in a river of holy love.

[Jesus said,] "My Father, who has given them to Me, is greater than all; and no one is able to snatch them out of My Father's hand" (John 10:29).

In the center of
God's hand
you find the center of
His will;
in the center of His will,
you find the center of
His peace;
in the center of His peace,
you find the center of
His love;
in the center of His love,
you find the center of
His heart.

Fret Buster 32

Kept by the Keeper

> The LORD is your keeper; the LORD is your
> shade at your right hand (Psalm 121:5).

God has no weaknesses and no place where He is vulnerable to attack. He is never helpless, defenseless, at risk, or in danger of a surprise attack. Nothing and no one can lead to His downfall. It is impossible for God to be defeated. This wonderful God is your keeper! He is your protector, shield, and fortress.

There is nothing that can separate you from Him, regardless of the battles you're in today. There is no separation between you and Your Captain, Your Warrior, and Your King. You march under Jesus's banner; you advance under His command; you conquer with the sword of His Word; you stand upon His authority; you resist under His rule. You are victorious because He is. You are strong because He is. You are an overcomer because He is.

Magnificence

All were astounded at the evidence of God's
mighty power and His majesty and magnificence (Luke 9:43 AMP).

Only God can turn a life from

- meaninglessness to purposefulness,
- barrenness to fruitfulness,
- heaviness to joyfulness,
- ugliness to loveliness,
- aimlessness to hopefulness,
- anxiousness to peacefulness

These and so much more declare His magnificence!

Fret Buster 33

Your own ears will hear him. Right behind you a voice will say, "This is the way you should go," whether to the right or to the left (Isaiah 30:21 NLT).

There are two things that often rob us of peace. One is "incomplete obedience to the will of God" and the second is "going beyond the will of God." It's important to go when God says "Go!" and it's equally important to stop when He says, "Stop!"

[The LORD says,] "I will instruct you and teach you in the way you should go; I will guide you with My eye" (Psalm 32:8).

[Jesus said,] "The sheep that are My own hear and are listening to My voice; and I know them, and they follow Me" (John 10:27 AMP).

Trust the Lord
for today's portion of:

daily bread
daily grace
daily strength
daily hope
daily joy, and
daily peace.

Fret Buster 34

Who Is Like Our God?

> You who have done great things; O God, who is like You? (Psalm 71:19).

There is no God like our God!
We don't need to help Him out for He is
   all-powerful.
We don't need to give Him solutions for
   He is all-wise.
We don't need to give Him explanations
   for He is all-knowing.
We don't need to wake Him up for He
   never slumbers or sleeps.
We don't need to hope that He will show
   up for He is always present.
We don't need to try to figure Him out for
   His ways are beyond finding out.
We don't need to make Him weapons of
   warfare for He knows no defeat.
We don't need to try to get His attention
   for His ears are open to our cries.

Focus...

> Not on the winds of opposition, but on
> the setting of the sail;
> Not on the howling of the storm, but on
> the voice of the Captain;
> Not on the darkness of the sea, but on the
> lighthouse on the shore;
> Not on the density of the fog, but on the
> true north of the compass;
> Not on the restlessness of the waves, but
> on the anchor that holds steady.

Fret Buster 35

Humble yourselves under the mighty hand of God, that He may exalt you in due time, *casting all your care upon Him,* for He cares for you (1 Peter 5:6-7).

Be full of confidence not in yourself or what you can do, but in the Lord and what He can do. Your life, once given to Him, is in His hands, not yours. Live in His strength, not yours. Depend on His resources, not your own.

Do not cast away your confidence, which has great reward (Hebrews 10:35).

How do you cast your care on Him?

- Get out your "fishing pole of faith."
- Tie a hook to the line on your fishing pole.
- Take all your cares and put them on a hook.
- Cast the line as far as you can into the sea of God's faithfulness.
- Cut the line and leave them out there.

Take
"I can't"
out of your vocabulary,
and replace it with
"God can!"

Fret Buster 36

Thou openest Thy hand, and satisfiest the desire of every living thing (Psalm 145:16 KJV).

Who considers these words enough? The hand of God being my chief provision and storehouse, is it not a shame to be anxiously careful for anything? Has the Lord all things in His hand? Then surely I shall receive what He has for me; none will be able to withhold it…you need not, says Christ, seek those other things; they shall be brought to you, if ye only abide in Me. If this does not comfort and strengthen us, nothing else will.

CARL BOGATZKY

I Only Need You, Lord…

I only need You, Lord, when the first light of dawn appears in the eastern sky; until the last golden hues of the sunset fade upon the western horizon. I only need You, Lord, when the night sky is over my head.

I only need You, Lord, when I rise up and when I sit down; when I go out and when I come in; when I am quiet and when I am active; when I am alone and when I am with others; when I am healthy and when I am ill; when I am up and when I am down; when I am on the go and when I need to wait.

I only need You, Lord, when my lungs need to breathe; when my blood needs to flow; when my body needs to move; when my muscles need to work; when my mind needs to think; when my heart needs to love.

I only need You, Lord, for as long as birds need flight; for as long as whales need the sea; for as long as clouds need moisture; for as long as wildflowers need raindrops; for as long as sunflowers need the summer sun.

I only need You, Lord, for this present moment; for the moment when You take me home; for all the moments in-between; and for all the moments ever after.

Fret Buster 37

> The peace of God, which surpasses all under-
> standing, will guard your hearts and minds
> through Christ Jesus (Philippians 4:7).

Perfect peace is not partial peace. Perfect peace is complete, full, unmixed. It is "shalom" peace—rich in blessings, well-being, and God's favor. It is peace of "good health" for the mind, the spirit, and the body. Perfect peace will keep you perfectly peaceful.

> You shall not go out with haste, nor go by
> flight; for the LORD will go before you, and
> the God of Israel will be your rear guard
> (Isaiah 52:12).

God's peace and calmness are marks of our walk when the Holy Spirit is in control of us—sanctifying our thoughts, guiding our steps, directing our decisions, prompting us to move at the right time, and assuring us that He goes before us.

> Let the peace of God rule in your hearts
> (Colossians 3:15).

God wants you
to move through this day with
a quiet heart,

an inward assurance
that He is in control,

a peaceful certainty
that your life is in His hands,

a deep trust
in His plan and purposes,

an abiding hope
in His promises,

and
a thankful disposition
toward all that He allows.

Fret Buster 38

Care will break the rest of the soul as much as sin does. And there is no hope that we should know the peace that passes all understanding till we have learned the art of shutting the door against the long train of burden-carrying thoughts that are always coming up the hill from the world beneath to fill our spirit with the ring of their feet and the clamor of their cries.

F.B. Meyer

We depend upon the Lord alone to save us. Only he can help us; he protects us like a shield (Psalm 33:20 TLB).

Let the Lord be the One—

- *you call on*: "I will call upon the LORD, who is worthy to be praised; so shall I be saved from my enemies" (Psalm 18:3).

- *you wait on*: "Those who wait on the LORD shall renew their strength" (Isaiah 40:31).

- *you feed on*: "[Jesus said,] 'I am the Bread of Life [that gives life—the Living Bread]…I [Myself] am this Living Bread that came down from heaven. If anyone eats of this Bread, he will live forever; and also the Bread that I shall give for the life of the world is My flesh (body)'" (John 6:48,51 AMP, brackets in original).

- *you depend on*: "We depend upon the Lord alone to save us. Only he can help us; he protects us like a shield" (Psalm 33:20 TLB).

Fret Buster 39

> I consider that the sufferings of this present time are not worthy to be compared with the glory which shall be revealed in us (Romans 8:18).

The peace that God gives you is not circumstantial peace. Being in a hammock at the beach on a warm, sunny day is not a picture of God's peace. Remember, the peace in your heart is *God's* peace. It's there because He's there, not because everything around you is calm and serene.

The peace of God is...

- given by Jesus
- different than the world's idea of peace
- able to quiet your troubled heart
- able to guard your heart and mind
- wonderful and doesn't need to be understood to be experienced

Even when you're
too weary
to stand,
the Lord
will
always
be there
to lean on!

Fret Buster 40

Wondering what to do? Don't try to—

- figure your way through
- reason your way through
- guess your way through
- feel your way through
- push your way through
- manipulate your way through
- fake your way through

What should you do?

- *Trust your way through!* "We do not know what to do, but our eyes are upon You" (2 Chronicles 20:12 AMP).

- *Pray your way through!* "Pray at all times (on every occasion, in every season) in the Spirit, with all [manner of] prayer and entreaty. To that end keep alert and watch with strong purpose and perseverance" (Ephesians 6:18 AMP, brackets in original).

- *Believe your way through!* "This is the victory that conquers the world, even our faith" (1 John 5:20 AMP).

- *Walk your way through!* "When you walk through the fire of oppression, you will not be burned up; the flames will not consume you. For I am the LORD, your God, the Holy One of Israel, your Savior" (Isaiah 43:2-3 NLT).

- *Praise your way through!* "So the people shouted when the priests blew the trumpets. And it happened when the people heard the sound of the trumpet, and the people shouted with a great shout, that the wall fell down flat" (Joshua 6:20).

Fret Buster 41

The government (the rule and reign of your life) is upon Jesus's shoulders. He hasn't placed any of it on yours. He has a plan and purpose for your life. He not only knows where He is taking you, but He also knows how to get you there.

> You will keep him in perfect peace, whose mind is stayed on You, because he trusts in You. Trust in the Lord forever, For in Yah, the Lord, is everlasting strength (Isaiah 26:3-4).

God won't say or do anything for the purpose of frustrating you, making you anxious, causing you panic, or filling you with fear.

The
government
will be upon
His shoulder.

(Isaiah 9:6)

Fret Buster 42

Even if everyone else is a liar, *God is true*.
As the Scriptures say about him, "You will
be proved right in what You say" (Romans
3:4 NLT).

Either

Either God is all-powerful or He is not. If He is not,
we are sunk. If He is, we have nothing to fear.

Either God is all-knowing or He is not. If He is
not, we'd better figure out what is best for us. If He is,
we can be confident He will not make mistakes with
our lives.

Either God is all-present or He is not. If He is not,
we need to find a way to protect and take care of ourselves. If He is, we can be assured His eye is watching
us, His hand is upon us, and His covering is over us.

Either God is the Father of mercies or He is not.
If He is not, we should work hard to find a way to
appease His wrath. If He is, we can, by faith, receive
the forgiveness He's provided for us through the shed
blood of His Son, Jesus Christ.

Upon His Shoulders, Close to His Heart

Jesus, your High Priest, carries you on the strength of His shoulders to bear you up in all your trials. He keeps you close to His heart with the deepest attention and affection. He represents you before the Father with compassionate and sympathetic understanding.

Jesus, your High Priest, strengthens you and helps you; upholds you and undergirds you; carries you and cares for you; represents you and remembers you. He is praying that you will be fruitful in everything by remaining within the will of God.

Fret Buster 43

> Do not fret…it only causes harm (Psalm 37:8).

If you don't have peace about what you're doing, stop doing it. Most likely it's not the right or best thing to do or it's not the right time.

> "I have the right to do anything," you say—but not everything is beneficial. "I have the right to do anything"—but not everything is constructive. No one should seek their own good, but the good of others (1 Corinthians 10:23-24).

COUNT

— on —

GOD

in *everything* you do,
in every *circumstance* you're in,
in every *need* you face,
in every *decision* you make.

Fret Buster 44

Has God ever left you?
Will He leave you now?

> He Himself has said, "I will never leave you…" (Hebrews 13:5).

Has He ever forsaken you?
Will He forsake you now?

> He Himself has said, "I will never leave you nor forsake you" (Hebrews 13:5).

Has He ever failed you?
Will He fail you now?

> Be strong, courageous, and firm; fear not nor be in terror before them, for it is the Lord your God Who goes with you; He will not fail you or forsake you (Deuteronomy 31:6 AMP).

Has He ever stopped watching over you?
Will He watch over you now?

The LORD keeps watch over you as you come and go, both now and forever (Psalm 121:8 NLT).

Has He ever turned His love away from you?
Will He turn away from you now?

The Lord appeared from of old to me [Israel], saying, Yes, I have loved you with an everlasting love; therefore with loving-kindness have I drawn you and continued My faithfulness to you (Jeremiah 31:3 AMP, brackets in original).

Has He ever ceased to be faithful?
Will He be faithful now?

The Lord is faithful and will strengthen you and protect you against the evil one (2 Thessalonians 3:3 GW).

Fret Buster 45

Keep and guard your heart with all vigilance and above all that you guard, for out of it flow the springs of life (Proverbs 4:23 AMP).

When an anxious thought comes knocking on the door of your mind, you can refuse it entrance. If you invite it in, it will have dinner with you, and if it has dinner with you, it will quickly move in and want to spend the night.

Believers have much to gather along the way, while doubters travel with empty baskets.

Without **faith**
it is *impossible*
to please [God],
for he who comes to God
must **believe** that He is,
and that He is a rewarder of
those who diligently seek
Him.

(Hebrews 11:6)

Fret Buster 46

Oh, taste and see that the LORD is good;
blessed is the man who trusts in Him!
(Psalm 34:8).

God is good to you! Enjoy the blessings that come from trusting Him.

His character is flawless, His worth is priceless, His power is endless, His faithfulness is ceaseless, His grace is boundless, His ways are blameless, His name is changeless, His blessings are countless, His glory is fadeless.

This Is the Day the Lord Has Made

Your theme song for the day is "Rejoice!"

"This is the day the LORD has made; we will
rejoice and be glad in it" (Psalm 118:24).

Today is a fresh start in His mercies. Live free from the cares of tomorrow.

"The reason I can still find hope is that I
keep this one thing in mind: the LORD's

mercy…His compassion is never limited. It is new every morning. His faithfulness is great"; so don't ever worry about tomorrow" (Lamentations 3:21-23 GW; Matthew 6:34 GW).

Carry hope in His promises all through the day. At night, God's faithfulness will be there to tuck you in.

"Be zealous for the fear of the LORD all the day"; "it is good to give thanks to the LORD, and to sing praises to Your name, O Most High…to declare your lovingkindness in the morning, and Your faithfulness every night" (Proverbs 23:18; Psalm 92:1-2).

Fret Buster 47

The Lord's presence in your life is not a small thing or a big thing—it is everything. The Lord's presence with you today is your rest!

He is…

- the guardian to keep you
- the shade to cover you
- the shield to protect you
- the warrior to defend you

He is…

- before you as your guide
- behind you as your guard
- beside you as your friend
- around you as your shelter
- above you as your watchman
- underneath you as your foundation

He is the peace that keeps you, the song that fills you, and the love that holds you through every moment of every day.

Should I be anxious
if God has all power?

Should I worry
if He knows all things?

Should I be afraid
if He is always present?

Should I doubt
if His promises are true?

Should I disobey
if His ways are best?

Should I strive
if He gives more grace?

Fret Buster 48

To Be Still...

Trust is a must.

> You will keep him in perfect peace, whose mind is stayed on You, because he trusts in You. Trust in the Lord forever, for in Yah, the Lord, is everlasting strength (Isaiah 26:3-4).

Rest works best.

> One handful of peace and quiet is better than two handfuls of hard work and of trying to catch the wind (Ecclesiastics 4:6 GW).

Peace brings release.

> He has redeemed my soul in peace from the battle that was against me (Psalm 55:18).

My Shepherd

There's a roadblock on my pathway,
And I fear that I will stray.
I must walk where You are leading,
Oh, my Shepherd, clear the way.
There's a pace that's very hectic,
That pursues me through the day.
How I long for quiet waters,
Oh, my Shepherd, lead the way.
There's a call to bring You glory,
But I'm just a jar of clay.
Lord, you know my every weakness,
Oh, my Shepherd, be the way.

Fret Buster 49

You can trust God's promises *absolutely*!

- He will never forget a promise He's made. (God knows all things.)

- He will never promise more than He is able to do. (With God, nothing is impossible.)

- He will never promise something He has no intention of doing. (God can't and won't lie.)

- He will never fail to fulfill a promise because of distractions. (With God there is no shadow of turning.)

Thinking "What will happen to me?" can move you away from God's grace by opening the door for your imagination to fill in the blanks with fear and worry.

You need grace for each issue you face. God is the source of all the grace you need, and He will not skimp or hold back any portion you need for today's journey. Tomorrow's grace will be yours tomorrow, and it also will be more than sufficient.

God is able
to make
all grace
abound
toward you.

(2 Corinthians 9:8)

Fret Buster 50

A Proclamation of Hope

> [We] rejoice in *hope* of the glory of God (Romans 5:2).

God, You are glorious! Because of who You are, I have hope in what You've promised to do. My future truly is as bright as the light on Your face that reflects it, as sure as the words upon Your lips that proclaim it, as powerful as the strength of Your right hand that performs to bring it about.

I am confident there are desirable things ahead because You are good. There are perfect things ahead because You are without fault. There are abundant things ahead because You are generous. There are undefiled things ahead because You are holy. There are amazing things ahead because You are wondrous. There are huge things ahead because Your heart is so big.

Peace Beyond Our Understanding

> Turn all your anxiety over to God because
> he cares for you (1 Peter 5:7 GW).

We don't need to know everything, have everything, or figure everything out to experience peace. In this life on earth, not everything will be known, understood, explained, or resolved. We need to let go of the idea that we must be in control of our lives, our families, and our future. God's control over us is enough. We can trust Him and walk in His peace.

Gaze into the mirror
    at the look upon your face.
Is it tense and full of worry
    or calm and full of grace?
Gaze into the mirror
    and see what's shining through.
Does it show a heart that's trusting
    in the One who cares for you?

Fret Buster 51

All He Is, He Is for You

Everything God is today He has always been; everything that He has always been He will always be.

Yesterday, God *was* with you. Today, God *is* with you. Tomorrow, God *will be* with you.

Was He your peace yesterday? He will be your peace today. Is He your peace today? He will be your peace tomorrow. Is He your provider today? He will be your provider tomorrow.

The psalmist wrote

> You will guard him and keep him in perfect and constant peace whose mind [both its inclination and its character] is stayed on You, because he commits himself to You, leans on You, and hopes confidently in You. So trust in the Lord (commit yourself to Him, lean on Him, hope confidently in Him) forever; for the Lord God is an everlasting Rock [the Rock of Ages] (Isaiah 26:3-4 AMP, brackets in original).

GOD IS
all that is *good*,
all that is *right*,
all that is *love*.

He's in control of
all that *concerns you!*

Fret Buster 52

Because…

Because God's kingdom is unshakeable,
we don't need to steady it.

Because God's provision of salvation is
complete, we don't need to improve it.

Because God's love is boundless, we don't
need to hoard it.

Because God's way is the best way, we
don't need to change it.

Because God's Word is truth, we don't
need to spin it.

Because God's hand can open any door,
we don't need to force it.

Because God's timing is perfect, we don't
need to rush it.

Because God's plan for us comes from a
Father's heart, we don't need to fight it.

He Giveth More Grace

When we have exhausted our store of endurance,
When our strength has failed ere the day is half done,
When we reach the end of our hoarded resources
    Our Father's full giving is only begun.

Fear not that thy need shall exceed His provision,
    Our God ever yearns His resources to share;
Lean hard on the arm everlasting, availing;
    The Father both thee and thy load will upbear.

His love has no limits, His grace has no measure,
    His power no boundary known unto men;
For out of His infinite riches in Jesus
    He giveth, and giveth, and giveth again.

ANNIE JOHNSON FLINT
(1866–1932)

Fret Buster 53

God's plan for you and care for you have nothing to do with chance, fate, or luck. His plan and care for you are solid. They're built upon a Rock—Jesus Christ—and established on truth, grounded in love, carried out by omnipotence, secured by providence, watched over by omnipresence, and determined by omniscience.

> We labor to take upon ourselves our weary burden, as if He were unable or unwilling to take it for us…Anxiety makes us doubt God's loving-kindness, and thus our love to Him grows cold, we feel mistrust, and thus grieve the Spirit of God…If through simple faith in His promise, we cast each burden as it comes upon Him, and are "anxious for nothing" because He undertakes to care for us, it will keep us close to Him, and strengthen us against much temptation.

C.H. SPURGEON,
DEVOTIONAL CLASSICS OF C.H. SPURGEON,
MORNING, MAY 26

I am the LORD,
the God of all flesh;
is there
ANYTHING
too hard for Me?

(Jeremiah 32:27 AMP)

Fret Buster 54

God's Word can be fully trusted!

- God does not speak lies (John 3:33).
- God cannot lie because He is holy (Psalm 89:35). God's holiness does not allow Him to lie.
- God's words are wise (Psalm 19:7). He never has to correct Himself or say He misspoke.
- God's words will not change (Psalm 119:89). He always has it right from the beginning!
- God's words are unshakeable. You can build your life upon them with absolute certainty and confidence (Matthew 7:24-25).

There is...

For every hectic workday, there is a quiet rest.
For every painful moment, there is a healing touch.
For every hurtful feeling, there is a deeper joy.
For every disappointment, there is a love that
    means so much.
For every doubting question, there is a
    guiding truth.
For every wounding heartache, there is a
    healing balm.
For every pressing deadline, there is a
    boundless grace.
For every tribulation, there is a peace that
    brings calm.

Fret Buster 55

God, the Healer of Hearts!

To the saddened heart, He pours the oil of
gladness;

To the discouraged heart, He brings a song
of hope;

To the lonely heart, He comes with the
nearness of His presence;

To the disappointed heart, He speaks a
promise of better things;

To the drifting heart, He secures the
anchor of His steadfast love;

To the wounded heart, He applies the
healing ointment of His grace;

To the soiled heart, He washes with the
rivers of His mercies;

To the troubled heart, He soothes with the
quiet strength of His peace.

"He heals the brokenhearted and binds up
their wounds [curing their pains and their
sorrows]" (Psalm 147:3 AMP, brackets in
original).

Beautiful

in all your splendor,

I yield

to you in full

surrender.

I take

your yoke,

there is no toil;

Lord,

pour on me your

healing oil.

Fret Buster 56

God created you, shaped you, and brought you into this world.

> Thus says the LORD, who created you, O Jacob, and He who formed you, O Israel…

God wants you to live without fear because the ownership of your life is in His hands.

> Fear not, for I have redeemed you…

God knows all about you. He knows your name and has set His claim upon you.

> I have called you by your name; you are Mine…

God is with you. He will bring you through every difficult circumstance and trial.

> When you pass through the waters, I will be with you; and through the rivers, they shall not overflow you. When you walk through the fire, you shall not be burned, nor shall the flame scorch you (Isaiah 43:1-2).

God has His eye upon you. You are precious to Him and well loved.

> Since you were precious in My sight, you have been honored, and I have loved you…

God is with you and doesn't want you to be in fear.

> Fear not, for I am with you…

God wants you to put your trust in Him and Him alone.

> [You are] My servant whom I have chosen, that you may know and believe Me, and understand that I am He. Before Me there was no God formed, nor shall there be after Me. I, even I, am the LORD, and besides Me there is no savior…

God is in absolute control.

> Indeed before the day was, I am He; and there is no one who can deliver out of My hand; I work, and who will reverse it? (Isaiah 43:4,5,10-11,13).

Fret Buster 57

You are seated with Christ. That means you are in a place of rest. To be seated with Him means you are in the place of *His* rest and the place of *His* victory. His call to you is not "Work hard to get to where I am," but rather, "Live today where I have placed you—with Me at My Father's right hand."

Are you waiting on God for an answer to
something you've prayed about?
Stay seated and rest in His answer.

Do you have a need you can't meet?
Stay seated and rest in His provision.

Are you facing a problem you can't solve?
Stay seated and rest in His wisdom.

Are you wondering how you're going to
make it through?
Stay seated and rest in His strength.

God
has brought us
back to life
together with
Christ Jesus
and has given us
a position
in heaven
with him.

(Ephesians 2:6 GW)

Fret Buster 58

I am not alienated
because You love *me.*

I am not unaided
because You help *me.*

I am not rejected
because You are for *me.*

I am not isolated
because You are with *me.*

I am not neglected
because You care *for me.*

I am not orphaned
because You are my Father.

I am not separated
because You are my portion.

I am not disheartened
because You are my future.

I am not unguarded
because You are my Defender.

I am not alarmed
because You are my God!

Fret Buster 59

Come to the Waters

Let us move with trusting hearts into the lush green meadow of God's will. Let us graze upon the promises that keep our souls from want. Let us listen to the voice of the Shepherd who never speaks an uncaring word. Let us drink of the waters that quench our deepest thirst. Let us simply and peacefully walk upon the pathway of good things. Let us be refreshed within the resting places that He prepares for us along the way.

The Lord is my shepherd;
    I shall not want.
He makes me to lie down in green pastures;
He leads me beside the still waters.
He restores my soul;
He leads me in the paths of righteousness
    for His name's sake
    (Psalm 23:1-3).

Lord,
I don't know
what will happen, and
I don't know
what will be…

But teach me to
live each
moment,
with a heart that's
worry free!

Fret Buster 60

Nothing Has Stopped in Heaven

Grace still abounds.
Mercies are still new this morning.
Blessings are still being poured out.
Prayers are still being heard and answered.
Promises are still being kept.
The love of God is still being shed abroad in
   our hearts.
Angels are still ministering.
Jesus is still interceding.
The Holy Spirit is still working.
God is still on the throne.
The return of the Lord is still on schedule!

Let the heavens rejoice, and let the earth be
   glad; and let them say among the nations,
   "The LORD reigns" (1 Chronicles 16:31).

The Painter

> I am certain that God, who began the good
> work within you, will continue his work
> until it is finally finished on the day when
> Christ Jesus returns (Philippians 1:6 NLT).

Life's like a landscape and God has the brush,
    His work is in progress, He's not in a rush.
Each stroke has a purpose, and nothing's by
        chance,
    to learn of His wisdom takes more than a
        glance.
The bird in the nest with its mouth opened wide,
    is just a reminder that God will provide.
Now look at the sheep in the meadow so green,
    the waters nearby are both calm and serene.
The parts of the picture which now seem unclear,
    will take on new meaning with each passing
        year;
Yes, God is still working in His perfect way,
    as He paints the landscape of your life each
        day.

Fret Buster 61

He is the God of the mountaintop and the valley.

On the mountaintop you see Him as the God of all glory. *In the valley you see Him as the God of all comfort.*

On the mountaintop you see Him as the Lord who reigns. *In the valley you see Him as the Shepherd who walks beside you.*

On the mountaintop you see Him as the Lord God omnipotent. *In the valley you see Him as your loving heavenly Father.*

A Personal Affirmation

I will not believe any lie that tells me God does not love me. I know I am loved. God doesn't say to me, "I love you because," or "I love you a little," or "I love you a lot," or "I love you on occasion," or "I love you when you're good," or "I love you every time you give Me a reason to love you." God loves me. Period! Because my life is hid with Christ in God…wherever I turn, I am facing love. Father, thank You for loving me!

GOD

is

LOVE.

(1 John 4:16)

Fret Buster 62

God also has highly exalted [Jesus Christ] and given Him the name which is above every name (Philippians 2:9).

How beautiful are the feet of those who preach the gospel of peace, who bring glad tidings of good things! (Romans 10:15).

It is only in the gospel of Jesus Christ that we find God's power to change a life, make a heart new, and bring peace. Jesus remains the only Savior from sin, the only Lord of life, the only King of glory, and the only Prince of peace.

Let us wave His banner, sing His song, and celebrate His presence. He is the hope we carry in our hearts through every sunrise and sunset, until the coming of that brighter day, when His shout will be heard, the trumpet will sound, God's kingdom will come, the righteous scepter will be extended from His hand, and He will reign over all.

Call Jesus

His footsteps are your guidance.
Call Him *the Way*.

His presence is your delight.
Call Him *Wonderful*.

His truth is your foundation.
Call Him *Rock*.

His will is your purpose.
Call Him *Lord*.

His kindness is your comfort.
Call Him *Shepherd*.

His promises are your hope.
Call Him *Faithful*.

His riches are your supply.
Call Him *Provider*.

His fellowship is your reward.
Call Him *Life*.

His heart is your home.
Call Him *Love*.

May the
Lord of
peace
Himself give you
peace
always in every way.
The Lord be with you.

(2 Thessalonians 3:16)

To read **Roy Lessin**'s
devotional blog, go to
www.meetmeinthemeadow.com